COLOSSAL CREATURE COUNT

Illustrated by Daniel Sanchez Limon

Edited by Jonny Marx
Designed by Jack Clucas
Cover design by John Bigwood

Buster Books

INTRODUCTION

Dr Christopher Taxonomy and Dr Michelle Ecology have been busy counting different species of animal for their groundbreaking scientific research.

The journey has taken them all over the world, but during their epic voyage disaster struck. Their notes were ruined in a huge storm.

Can you help the doctors find, and correctly tally, the creatures in every scene?

Dr Christopher Taxonomy

Dr Michelle Ecology

INSTRUCTIONS

1. Each habitat includes a checklist showing the animals you need to count and boxes to write your answers in.

2. Add up all of your answers. Does your total match the number in the total box that the doctors wrote down?

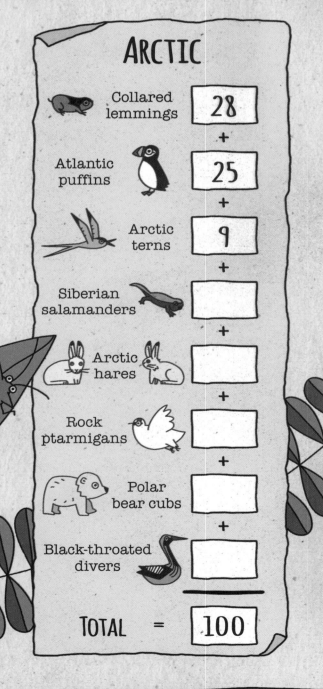

ARCTIC

Collared lemmings	28
Atlantic puffins	25
Arctic terns	9
Siberian salamanders	
Arctic hares	
Rock ptarmigans	
Polar bear cubs	
Black-throated divers	

TOTAL = 100

ARCTIC

Collared lemmings	28
Atlantic puffins	25
Arctic terns	9
Siberian salamanders	5
Arctic hares	11
Rock ptarmigans	10
Polar bear cubs	6
Black-throated divers	6

TOTAL = 100

3. If your total doesn't match, you'll have to start again, because you won't know which animals you have counted incorrectly!

STAR SPOTS

There are 18 extra-rare animals to spot throughout the book. Can you find them all and tick them off?

Common agouti 	Blobfish 	Scorpionfish 	Purple frog 	Crocodile icefish 
Pine marten 	Snub-nosed monkey 	Leaf-tailed gecko 	Red-lipped batfish 	Harlequin duck 
Natterjack toad 	Marbled lungfish 	Black beauty stick insect 	Great grey owl 	Cassowary 
Collared lizard 	Elephant shrew 	Species unknown 		

You will find all the answers in the back of the book.

There are 18 different habitats to explore:

River Nile
Yellowstone
Under the Sea
Australian Outback
Antarctica
European Woods

Peruvian Jungle
Himalayas
Amazon Rainforest
Galápagos Islands
African Savanna
Chihuahuan Desert

Great Barrier Reef
Indian Jungle
Arctic
British Pond
Madagascar
Abyss

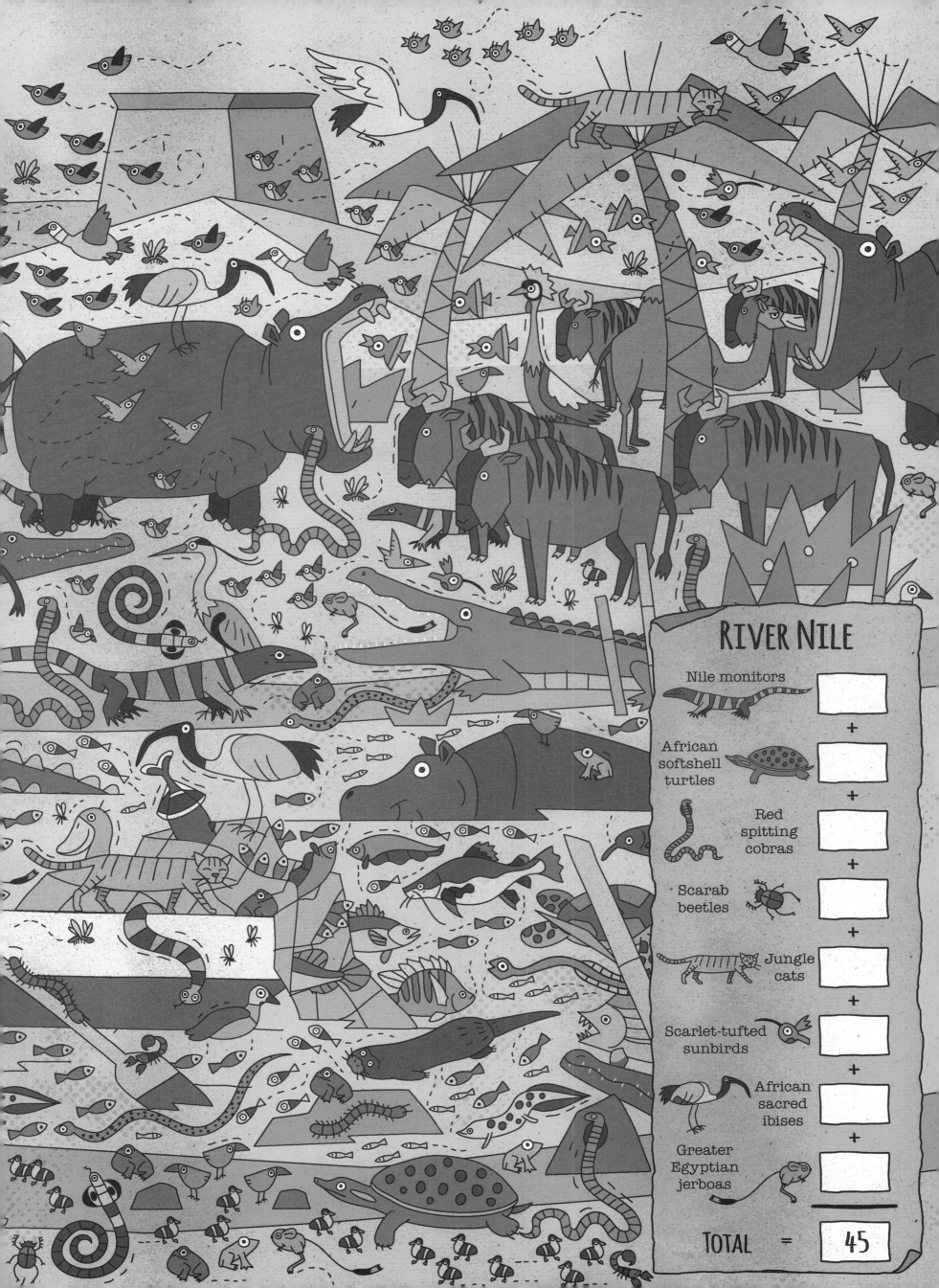

RIVER NILE

Nile monitors

African softshell turtles

+

Red spitting cobras

+

Scarab beetles

+

Jungle cats

+

Scarlet-tufted sunbirds

+

African sacred ibises

+

Greater Egyptian jerboas

TOTAL = 45

YELLOWSTONE

Animal		Count
Snowshoe hares		
Mallards		
American badgers		
Burrowing owls		
Townsend's big-eared bats		
American martens		
Yellowstone cutthroat trout		
American red squirrels		
TOTAL =		**55**

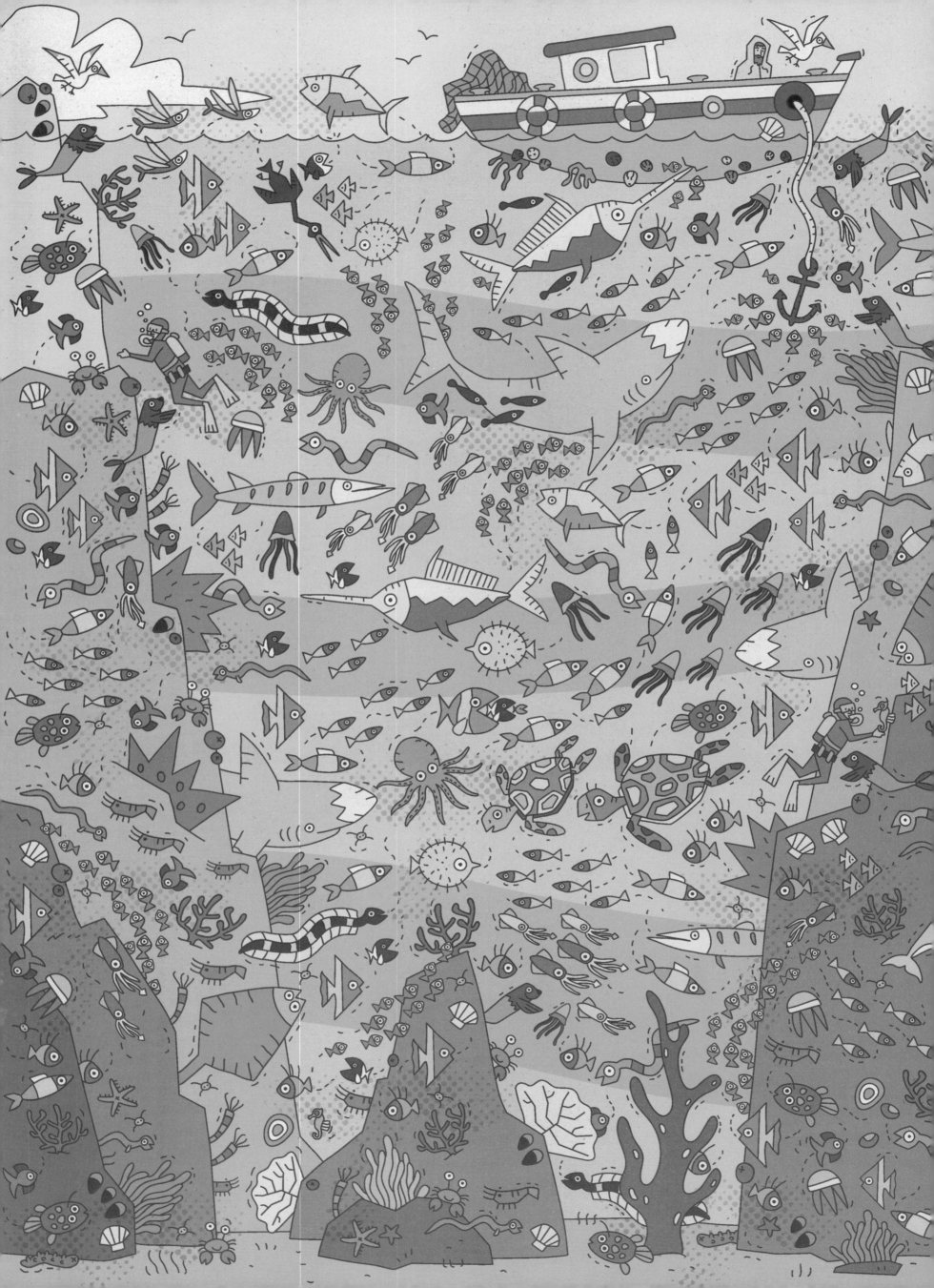

UNDER THE SEA

Brown fur seals		
	+	
Reef squid		
	+	
Jellyfish		
	+	
Red rock crabs		
	+	
Lined seahorses		
	+	
Royal angelfish		
	+	
Peppermint shrimp		
	+	
Long-spine porcupinefish		
TOTAL	=	125

AUSTRALIAN OUTBACK

Eastern brown snakes

+

Numbats

+

Thorny devils

+

Bilbies

+

Huntsman spiders

+

Quokkas

+

Blue-winged kookaburras

+

Australian pelicans

TOTAL = 50

ANTARCTICA

Emperor penguins	
+	
Wandering albatrosses	
+	
Chinstrap penguins	
+	
Macaroni penguins	
+	
Giant petrels	
+	
Gentoo penguins	
+	
King crabs	
+	
Antarctic toothfish	

TOTAL = 100

EUROPEAN WOODS

European hedgehogs		
	+	
Common shrews		
	+	
Common blue damselflies		
	+	
Common adders		
	+	
Grey field slugs		
	+	
Least weasels		
	+	
Black garden ants		
	+	
Brown garden snails		

TOTAL = 75

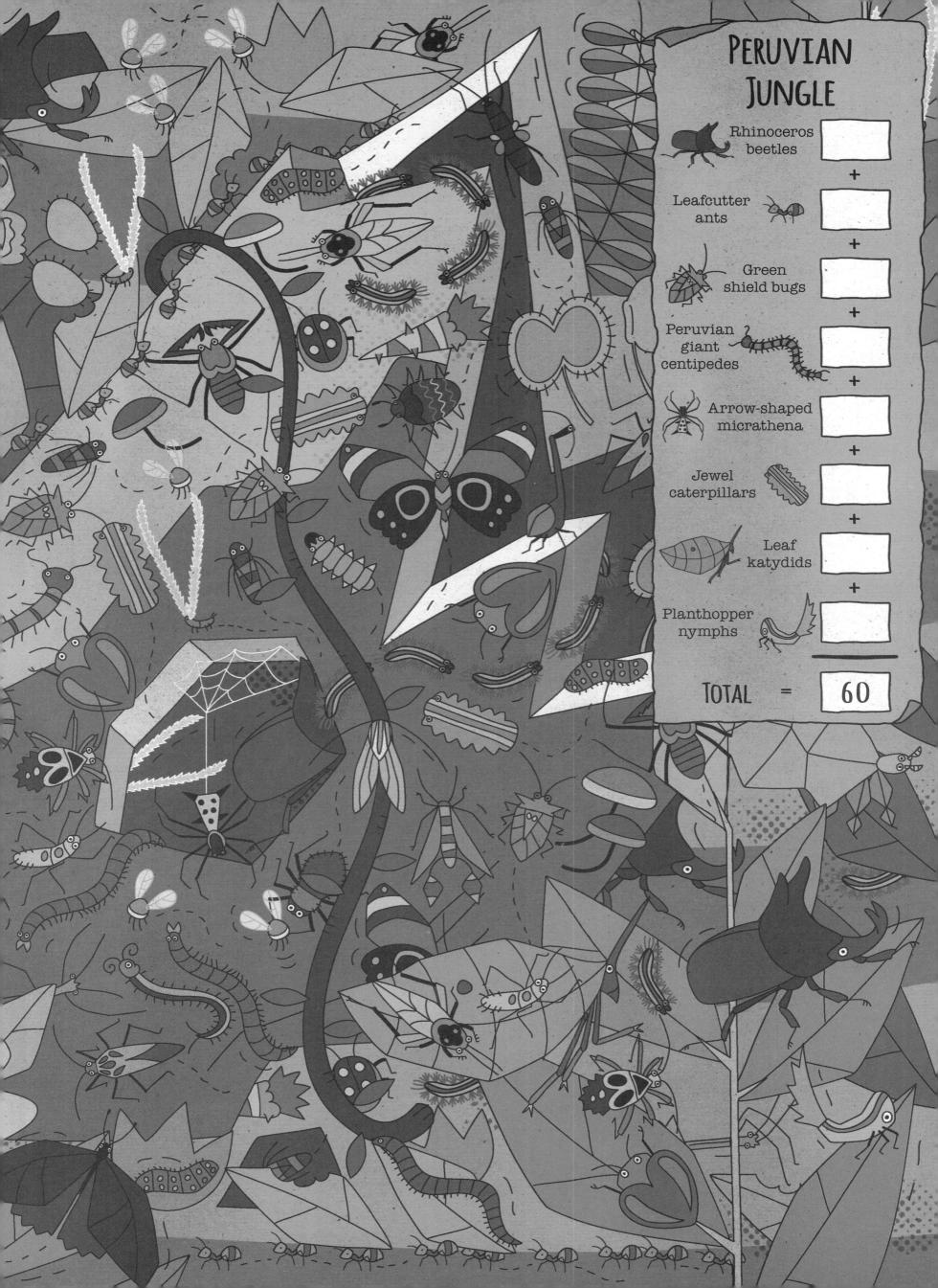

PERUVIAN JUNGLE

Rhinoceros beetles		
+		
Leafcutter ants		
+		
Green shield bugs		
+		
Peruvian giant centipedes		
+		
Arrow-shaped micrathena		
+		
Jewel caterpillars		
+		
Leaf katydids		
+		
Planthopper nymphs		

TOTAL = 60

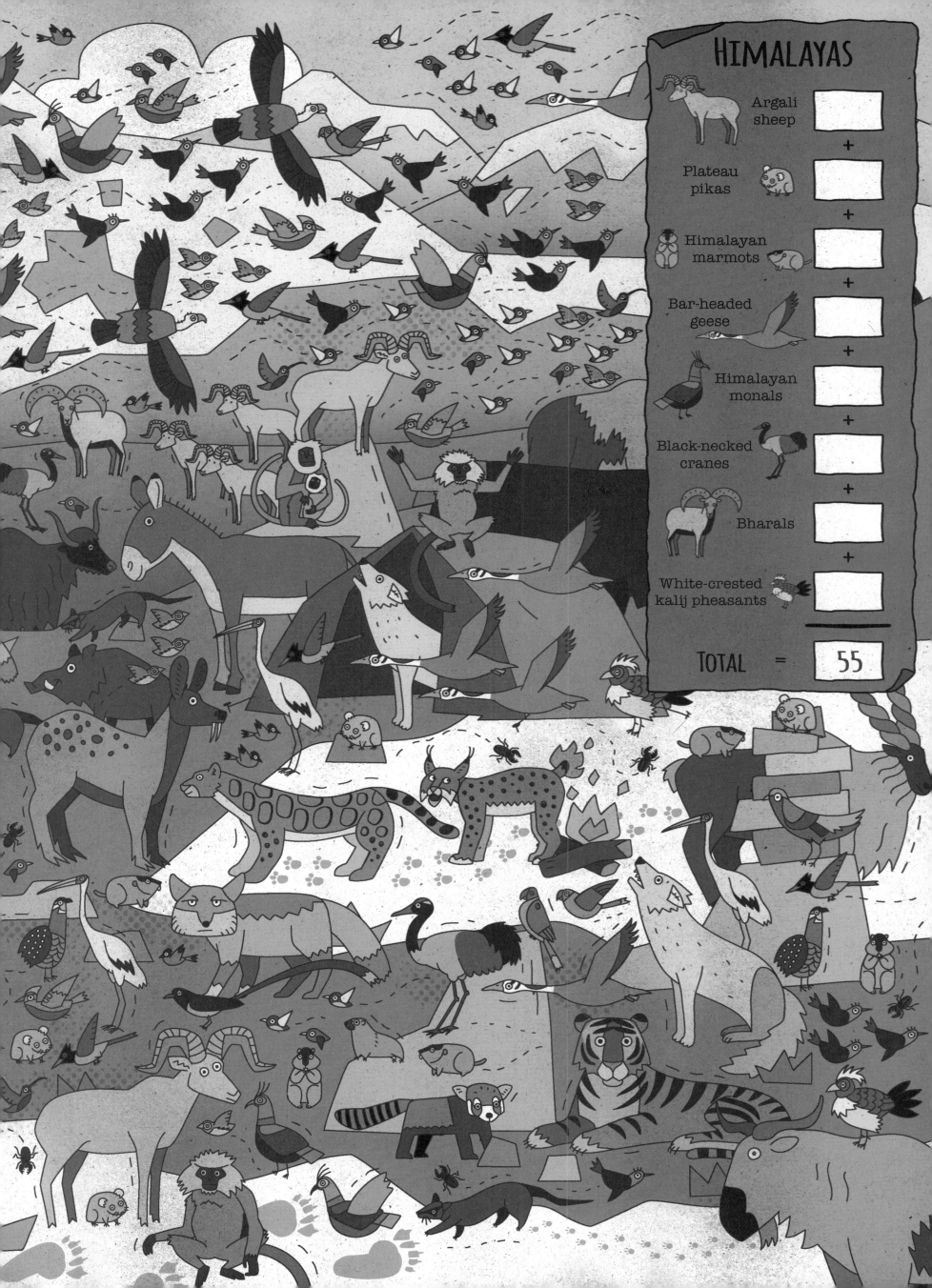

HIMALAYAS

Animal	Count
Argali sheep	
Plateau pikas	
Himalayan marmots	
Bar-headed geese	
Himalayan monals	
Black-necked cranes	
Bharals	
White-crested kalij pheasants	
TOTAL =	**55**

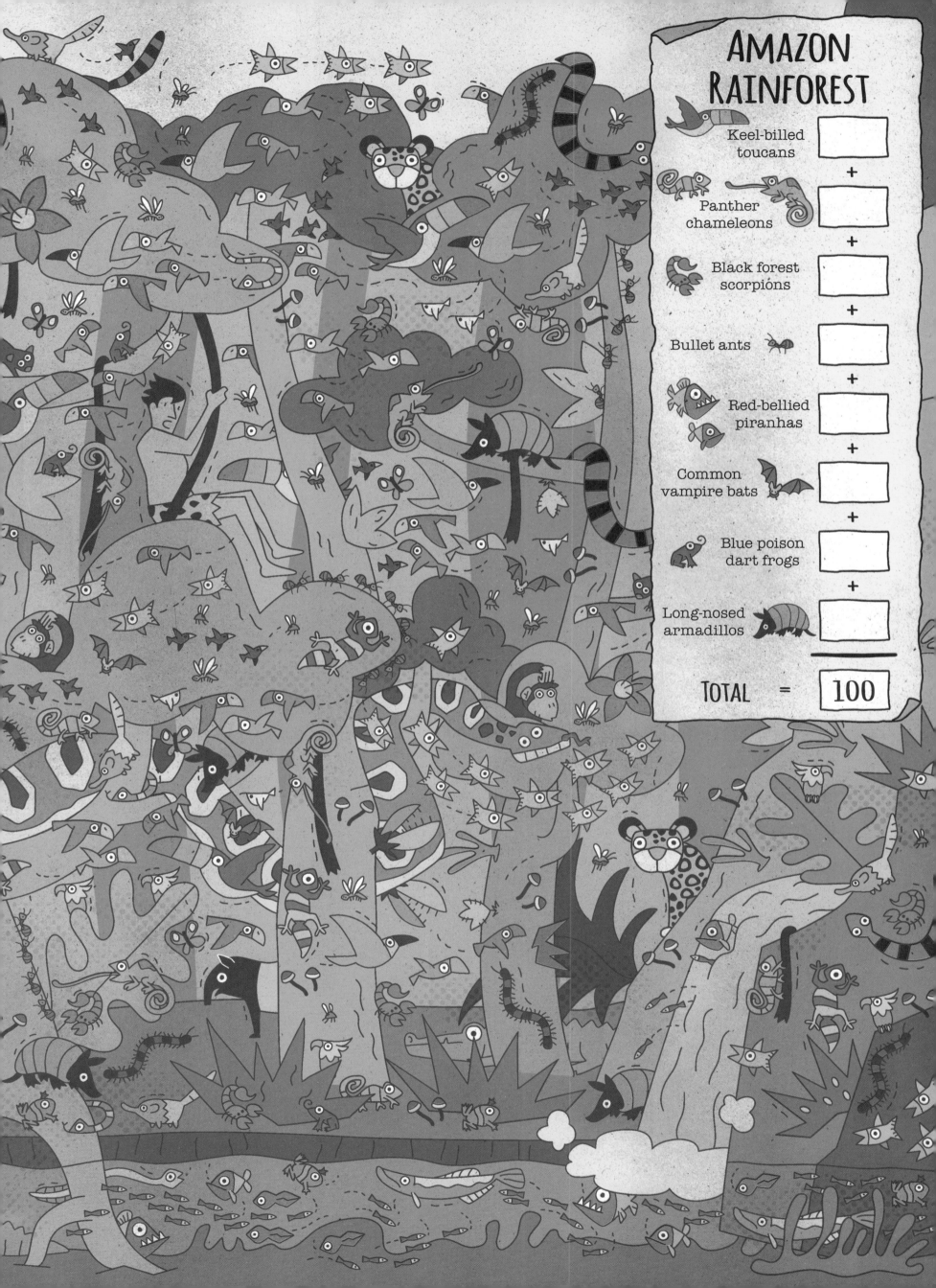

AMAZON RAINFOREST

Keel-billed toucans	
+	
Panther chameleons	
+	
Black forest scorpions	
+	
Bullet ants	
+	
Red-bellied piranhas	
+	
Common vampire bats	
+	
Blue poison dart frogs	
+	
Long-nosed armadillos	

TOTAL = 100

GALÁPAGOS ISLANDS

Marine iguanas	
+	
Sally Lightfoot crabs	
+	
Red-footed boobies	
+	
Lava lizards	
+	
Yellow warblers	
+	
Flightless cormorants	
+	
Magnificent frigatebirds	
+	
Hoary bats	

TOTAL = **75**

AFRICAN SAVANNA

White-headed vultures	
+	
Leopard tortoises	
+	
Aardvarks	
+	
Meerkats	
+	
Mosquitoes	
+	
Hamerkops	
+	
Puff adders	
+	
Mandrills	
TOTAL =	65

CHIHUAHUAN DESERT

Monarch butterflies	
+ Greater roadrunners	
+ Mexican redknee tarantulas	
+ Chihuahuan black-headed snakes	
+ Horned lizards	
+ Greater earless lizards	
+ Mexican prairie dogs	
+ Gila monsters	

TOTAL = 55

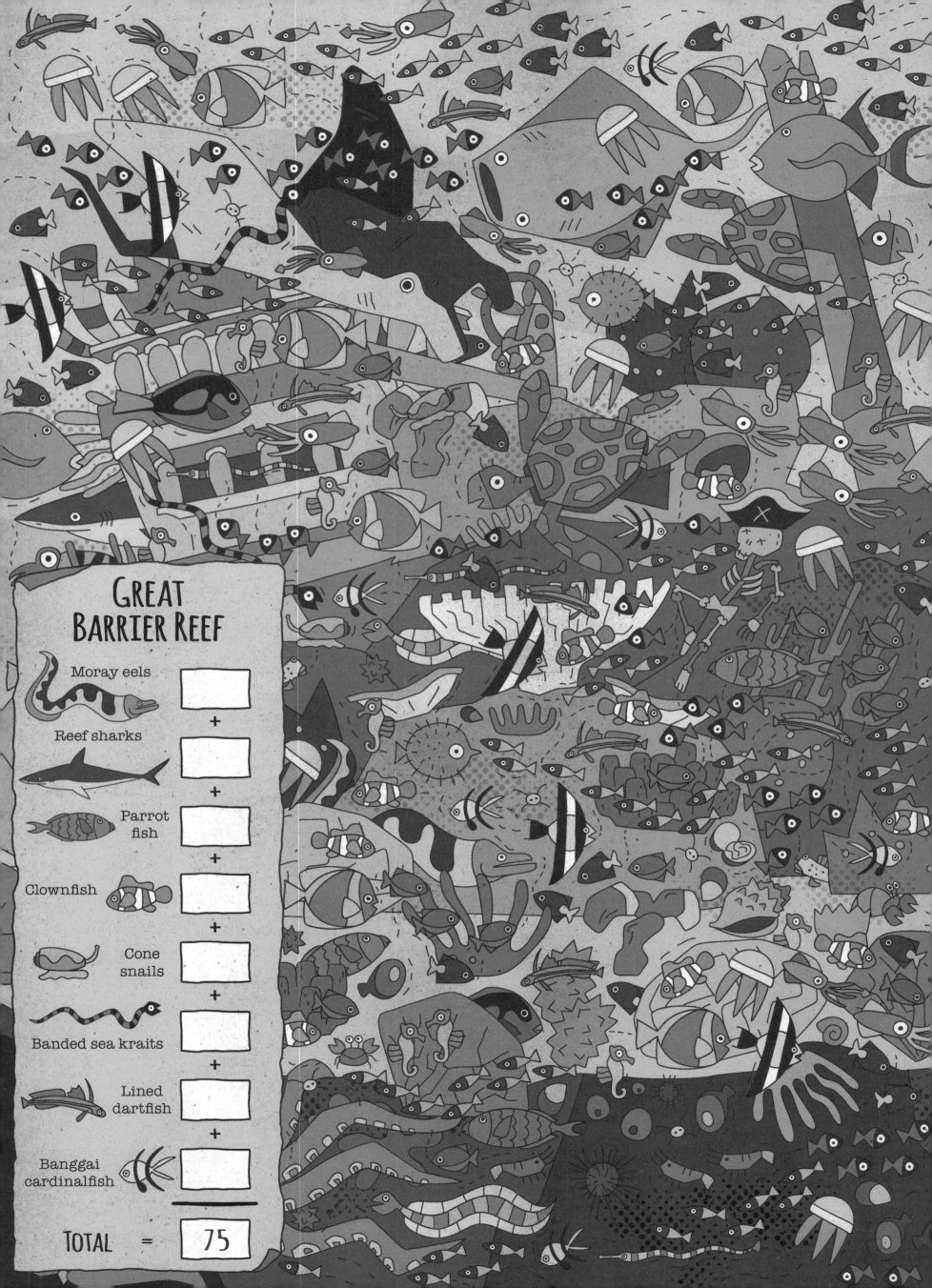

GREAT BARRIER REEF

Moray eels

[ ]

+

Reef sharks

[ ]

+

Parrot fish

[ ]

+

Clownfish

[ ]

+

Cone snails

[ ]

+

Banded sea kraits

[ ]

+

Lined dartfish

[ ]

+

Banggai cardinalfish

[ ]

TOTAL = 75

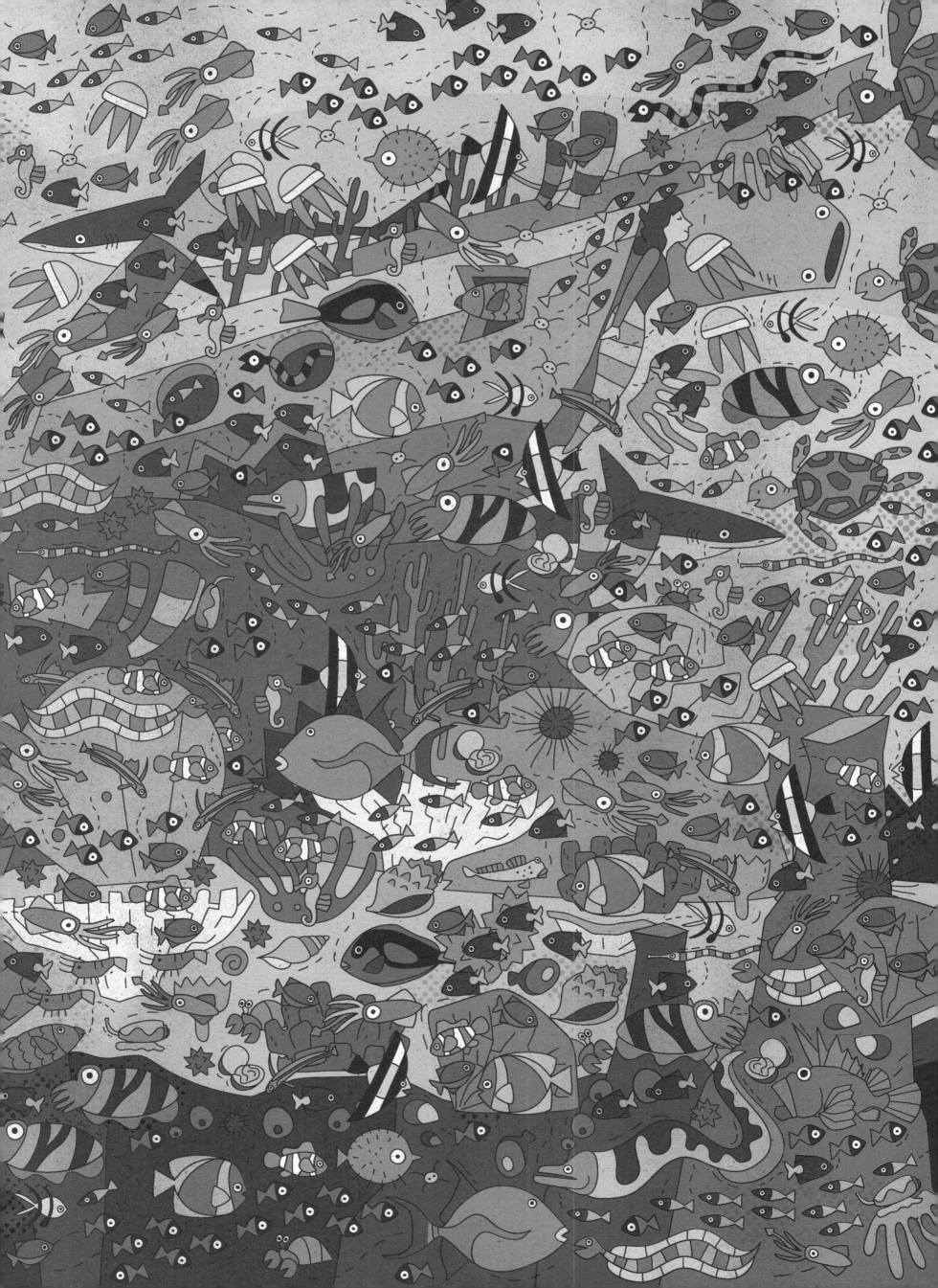

INDIAN JUNGLE

Animal	Count
Dholes	
Tiger centipedes	+
Jayaram's bush frogs	+
Grey langurs	+
Indian cobras	+
Arunachal macaques	+
Shikras	+
Golden langurs	+
TOTAL =	**45**

ARCTIC

Collared lemmings		
	+	
Atlantic puffins		
	+	
Arctic terns		
	+	
Siberian salamanders		
	+	
Arctic hares		
	+	
Rock ptarmigans		
	+	
Polar bear cubs		
	+	
Black-throated divers		
TOTAL =	100	

BRITISH POND

Seven-spot ladybirds		
	+	
Lesser water boatmen		
	+	
Black tadpoles with legs		
	+	
Great diving beetles		
	+	
Whirligig beetles		
	+	
Three-spined sticklebacks		
	+	
Yellow perch		
	+	
Common minnows		

TOTAL = 60

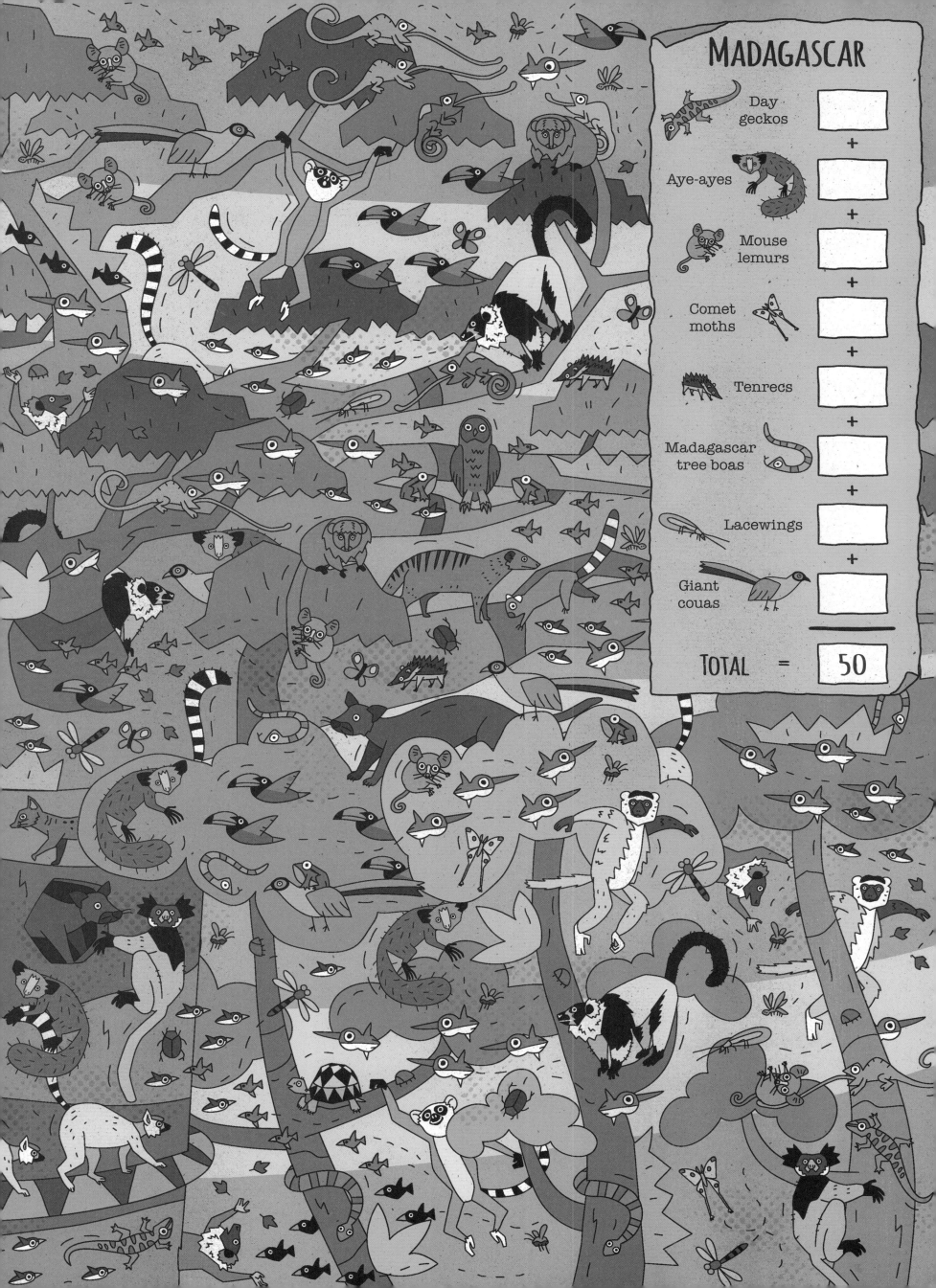

MADAGASCAR

Day geckos	
+	
Aye-ayes	
+	
Mouse lemurs	
+	
Comet moths	
+	
Tenrecs	
+	
Madagascar tree boas	
+	
Lacewings	
+	
Giant couas	

TOTAL = 50

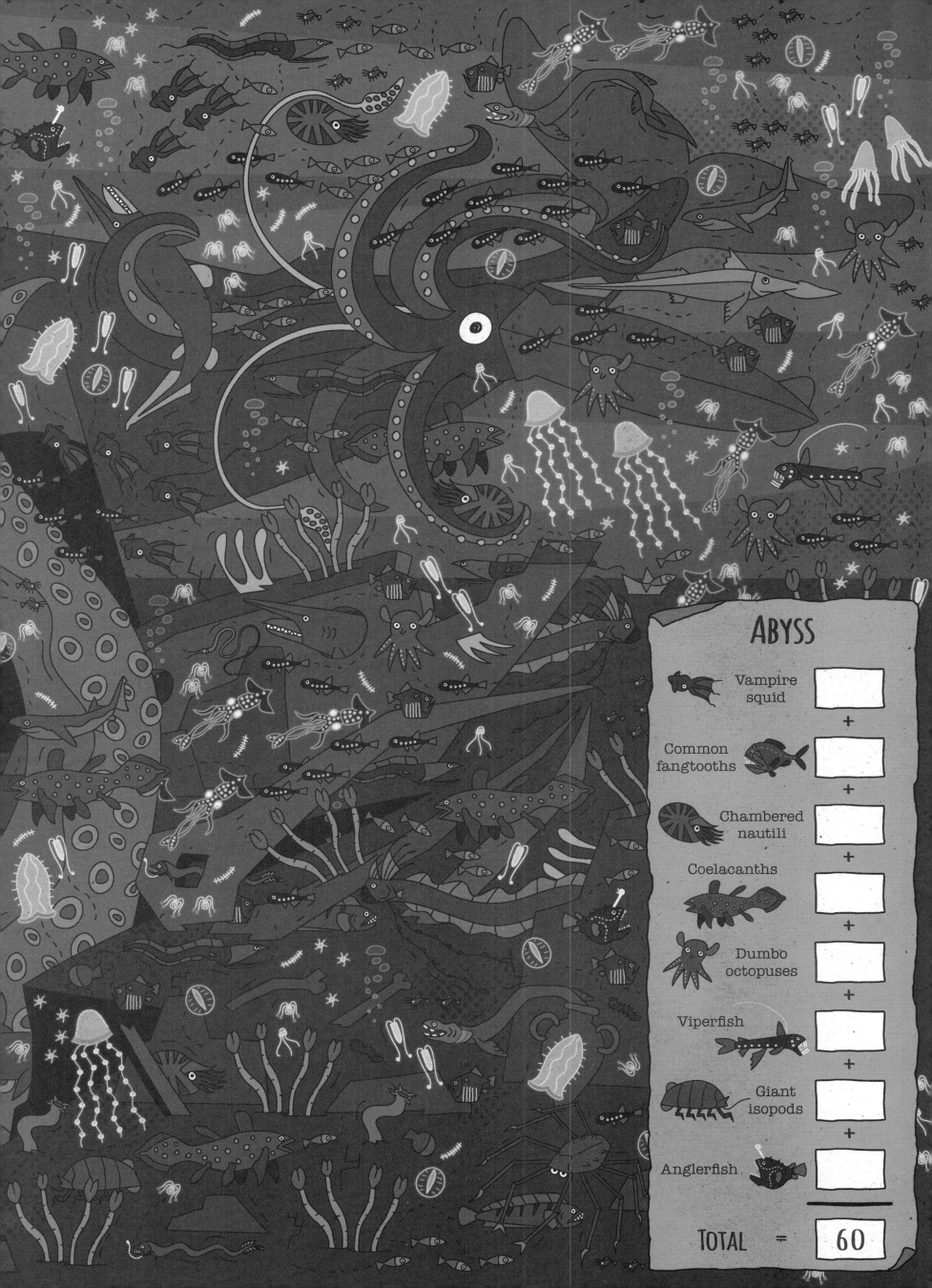

ABYSS

Vampire squid		
	+	
Common fangtooths		
	+	
Chambered nautili		
	+	
Coelacanths		
	+	
Dumbo octopuses		
	+	
Viperfish		
	+	
Giant isopods		
	+	
Anglerfish		
TOTAL	=	60

Answers

RIVER NILE

Animal	Count
Nile monitors	5
African softshell turtles	+ 3
Red spitting cobras	+ 7
Scarab beetles	+ 6
Jungle cats	+ 4
Scarlet-tufted sunbirds	+ 6
African sacred ibises	+ 9
Greater Egyptian jerboas	+ 5
TOTAL =	**45**

YELLOWSTONE

Animal	Count
Snowshoe hares	5
Mallards	+ 13
American badgers	+ 5
Burrowing owls	+ 6
Townsend's big-eared bats	+ 10
American martens	+ 4
Yellowstone cutthroat trout	+ 5
American red squirrels	+ 7
TOTAL =	**55**

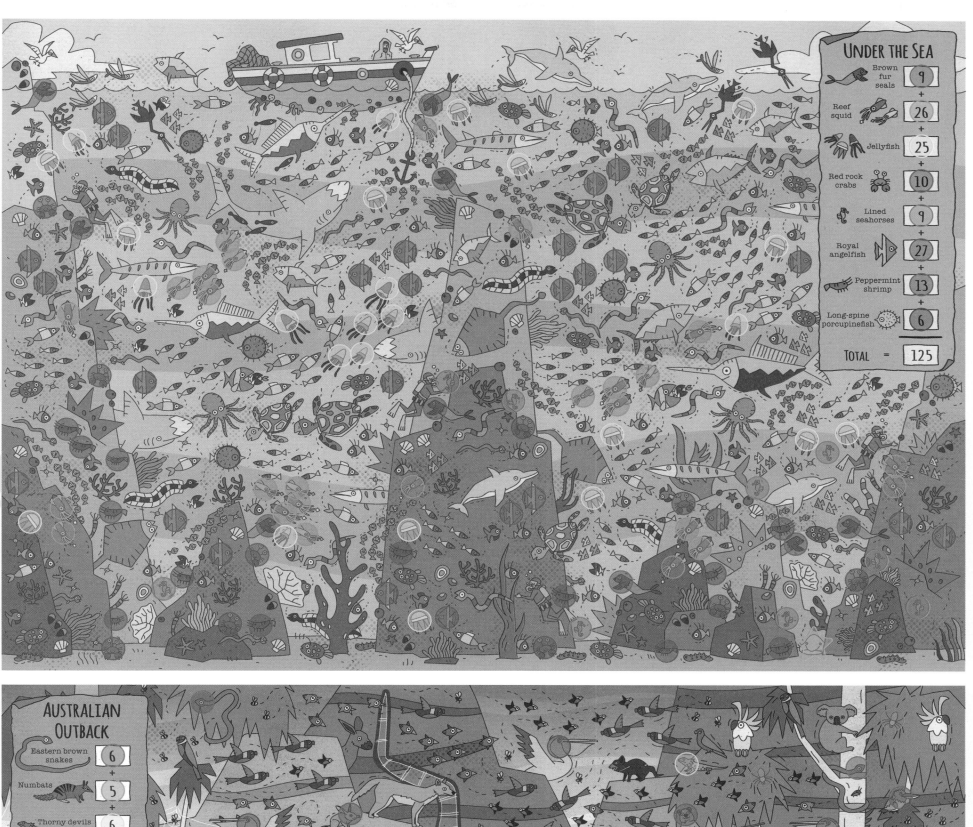

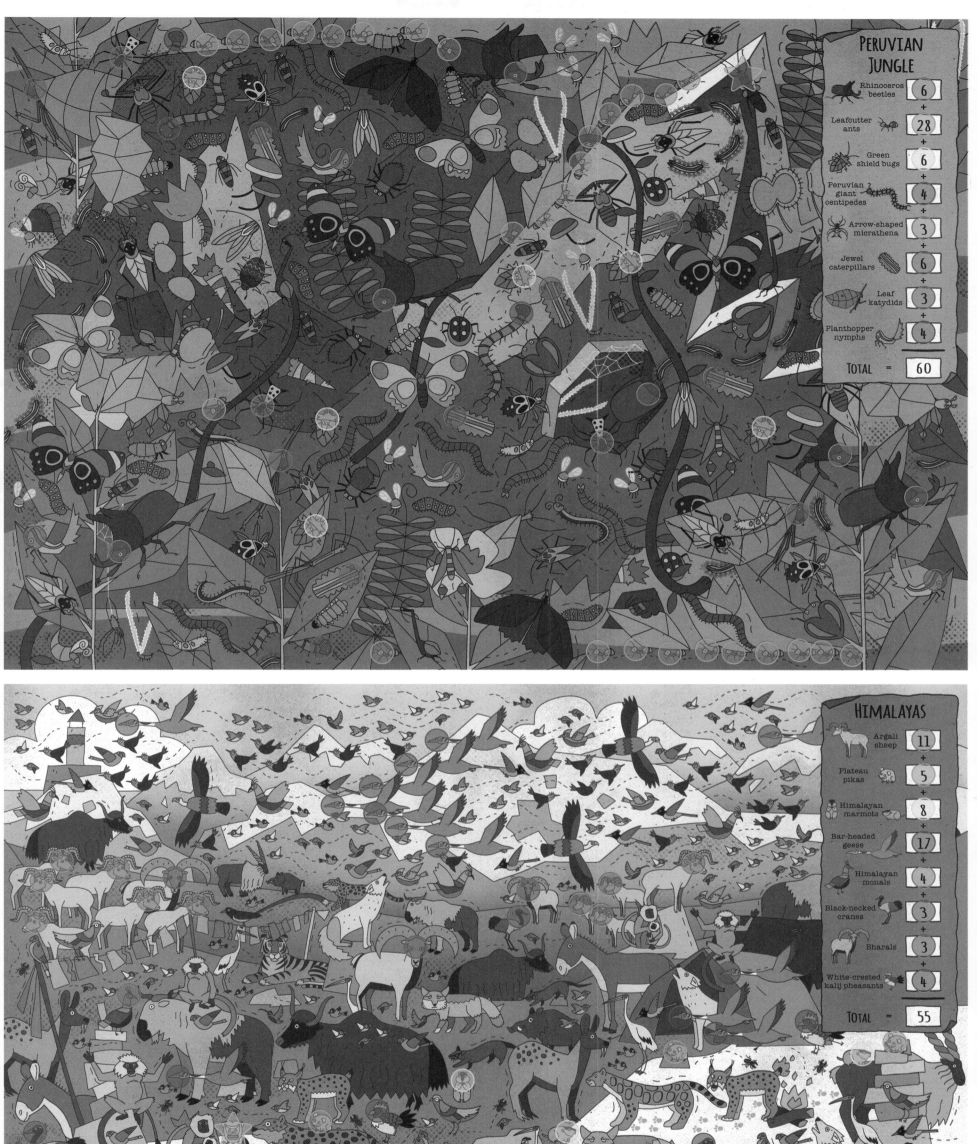

PERUVIAN JUNGLE

Rhinoceros beetles	6	+
Leafcutter ants	28	+
Green shield bugs	6	+
Peruvian giant centipedes	4	+
Arrow-shaped micrathena	3	+
Jewel caterpillars	6	+
Leaf katydids	3	+
Planthopper nymphs	4	
TOTAL =	60	

HIMALAYAS

Argali sheep	11	+
Plateau pikas	5	+
Himalayan marmots	8	+
Bar-headed geese	17	+
Himalayan monals	4	+
Black-necked cranes	3	+
Bharals	3	+
White-crested kalij pheasants	4	
TOTAL =	55	

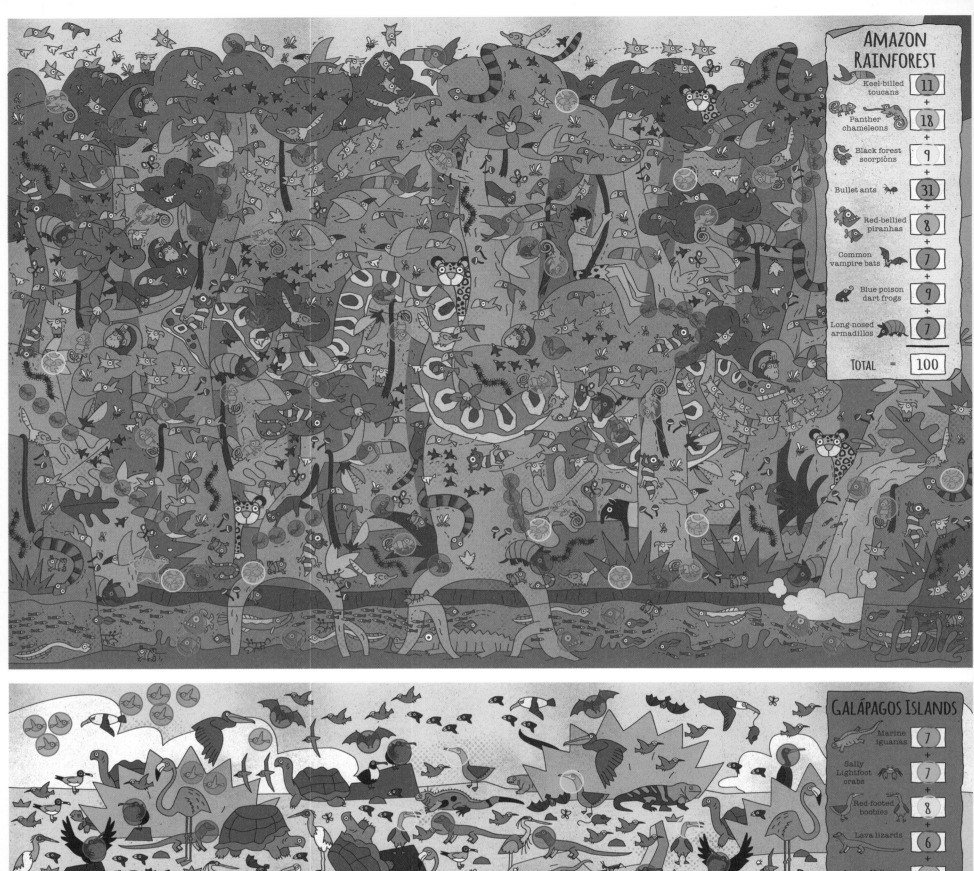

AMAZON RAINFOREST

Keel-billed toucans	11	
	+	
Panther chameleons	18	
	+	
Black forest scorpions	9	
	+	
Bullet ants	31	
	+	
Red-bellied piranhas	8	
	+	
Common vampire bats	7	
	+	
Blue poison dart frogs	9	
	+	
Long-nosed armadillos	7	
TOTAL	**=**	**100**

GALÁPAGOS ISLANDS

Marine iguanas	7
	+
Sally Lightfoot crabs	7
	+
Red-footed boobies	8
	+
Lava lizards	6
	+
Yellow warblers	28
	+
Flightless cormorants	6
	+
Magnificent frigatebirds	7
	+
Hoary bats	6
TOTAL	**= 75**

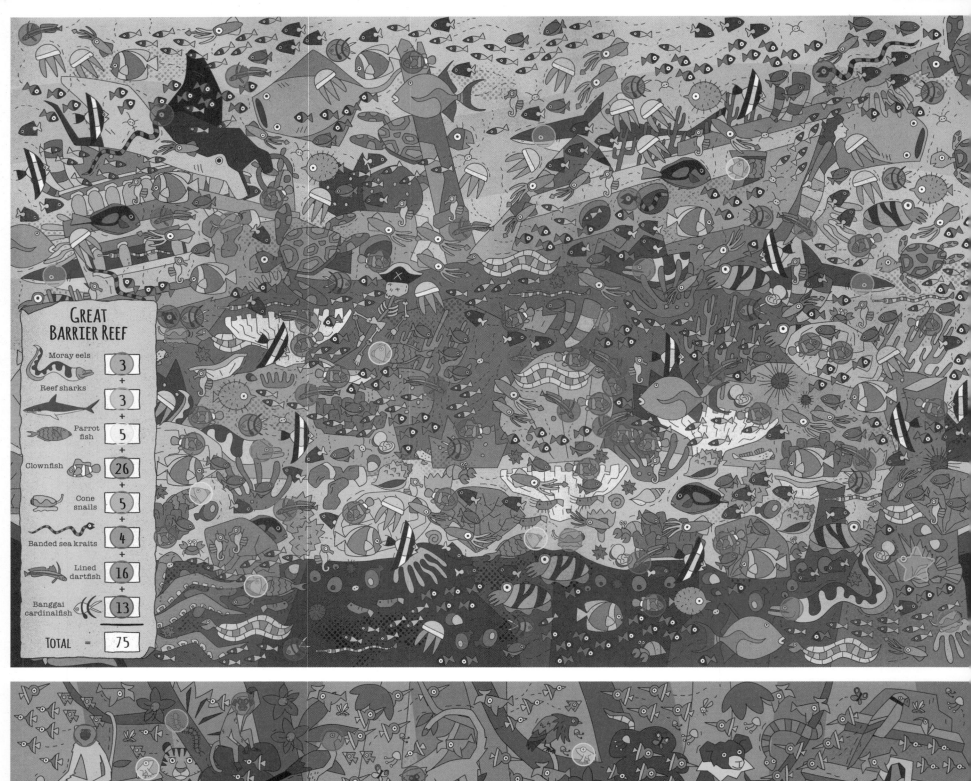

GREAT BARRIER REEF

Moray eels	3	
Reef sharks	+ 3	
Parrot fish	+ 5	
Clownfish	+ 26	
Cone snails	+ 5	
Banded sea kraits	+ 4	
Lined dartfish	+ 16	
Banggai cardinalfish	+ 13	
TOTAL =	**75**	

INDIAN JUNGLE

Dholes	6	
Tiger centipedes	+ 8	
Jayaram's bush frogs	+ 9	
Grey langurs	+ 6	
Indian cobras	+ 4	
Arunachal macaques	+ 5	
Shikras	+ 3	
Golden langurs	+ 4	
TOTAL =	**45**	

ARCTIC

Collared lemmings	28	
Atlantic puffins	25	+
Arctic terns	9	+
Siberian salamanders	5	+
Arctic hares	11	+
Rock ptarmigans	10	+
Polar bear cubs	6	+
Black-throated divers	6	+
TOTAL	**100**	=

BRITISH POND

Seven-spot ladybirds	7	
Lesser water boatmen	3	+
Black tadpoles with legs	11	+
Great diving beetles	10	+
Whirligig beetles	9	+
Three-spined sticklebacks	5	+
Yellow perch	6	+
Common minnows	9	+
TOTAL	**60**	=

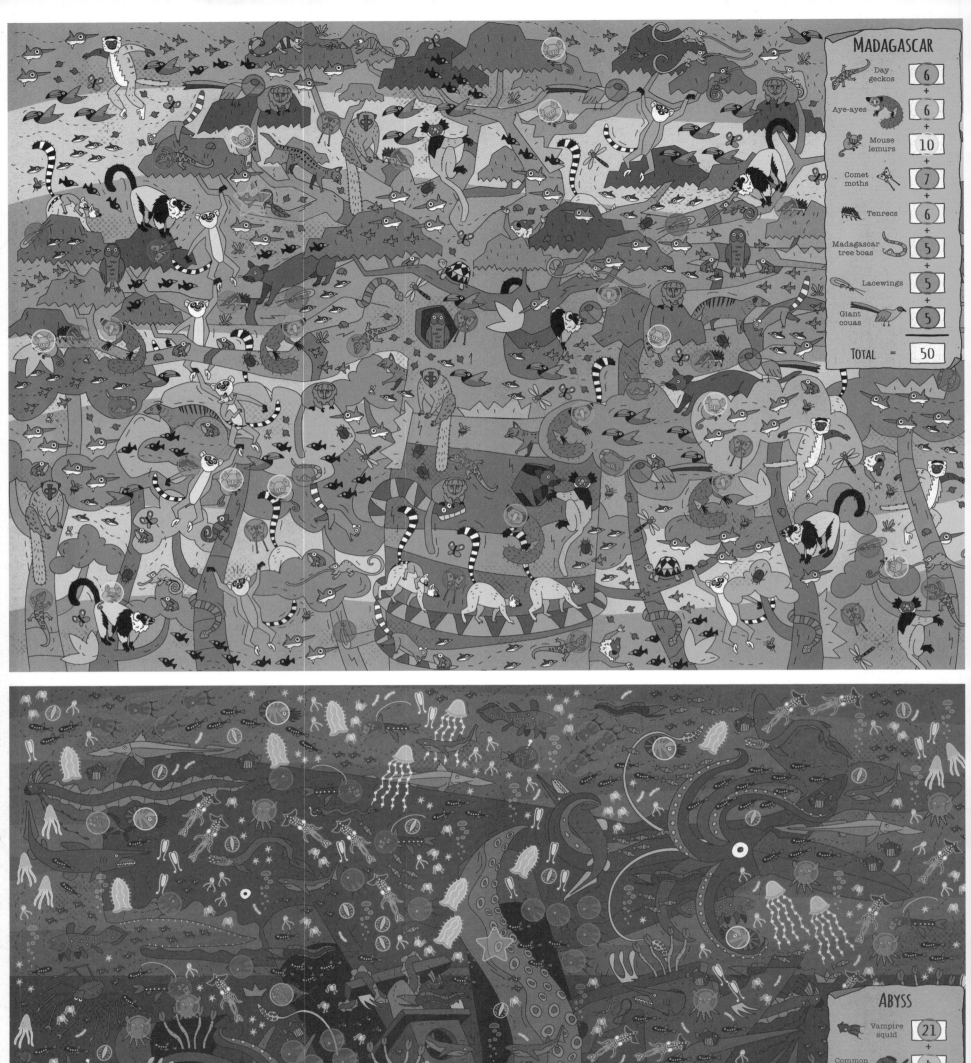

MADAGASCAR

Day geckos		6
Aye-ayes		+ 6
Mouse lemurs		+ 10
Comet moths		+ 7
Tenrecs		+ 6
Madagascar tree boas		+ 5
Lacewings		+ 5
Giant couas		+ 5
TOTAL	=	50

ABYSS

Vampire squid		21
Common fangtooths		+ 4
Chambered nautili		+ 6
Coelacanths		+ 6
Dumbo octopuses		+ 11
Viperfish		+ 5
Giant isopods		+ 4
Anglerfish		+ 3
TOTAL	=	60